# Bottlenose Dolphins

**by Grace Hansen**

Abdo
ANIMAL FRIENDS
Kids

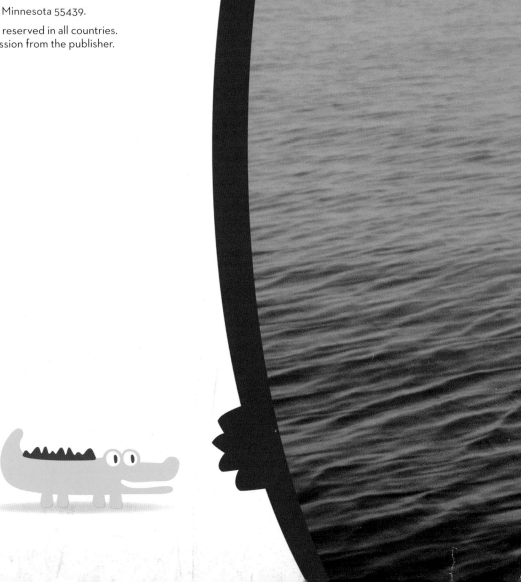

**abdopublishing.com**

Published by Abdo Kids, a division of ABDO, PO Box 398166, Minneapolis, Minnesota 55439.

Copyright © 2016 by Abdo Consulting Group, Inc. International copyrights reserved in all countries.
No part of this book may be reproduced in any form without written permission from the publisher.

Printed in the United States of America, North Mankato, Minnesota.

052015

092015

 THIS BOOK CONTAINS
RECYCLED MATERIALS

Photo Credits: iStock, Science Source, Shutterstock

Production Contributors: Teddy Borth, Jennie Forsberg, Grace Hansen

Design Contributors: Laura Rask, Dorothy Toth

Library of Congress Control Number: 2014960325

Cataloging-in-Publication Data

Hansen, Grace.

 Bottlenose dolphins / Grace Hansen.

  p. cm. -- (Animal friends)

 ISBN 978-1-62970-891-1

 Includes index.

 1. Bottlenose dolphin--Juvenile literature.   I. Title.

 599.53'3--dc23

                    2014960325

# Table of Contents

## Bottlenose Dolphins

Bottlenose dolphins live in the ocean. They like warmer waters.

4

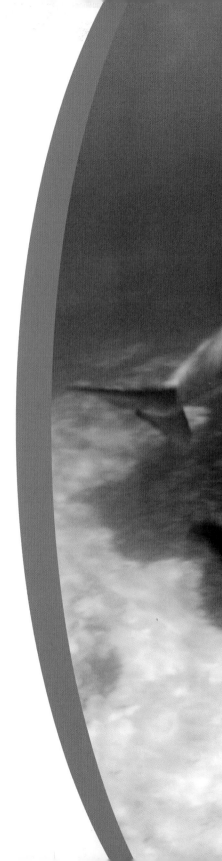

They live in groups. These groups are called **pods**. There are usually 2 to 15 members.

## Food

Bottlenose dolphins eat shrimp and fish. They also eat squid. They catch food with their sharp teeth.

9

## Body Parts

Bottlenose dolphins have smooth skin. It feels like rubber. They do not have any hair.

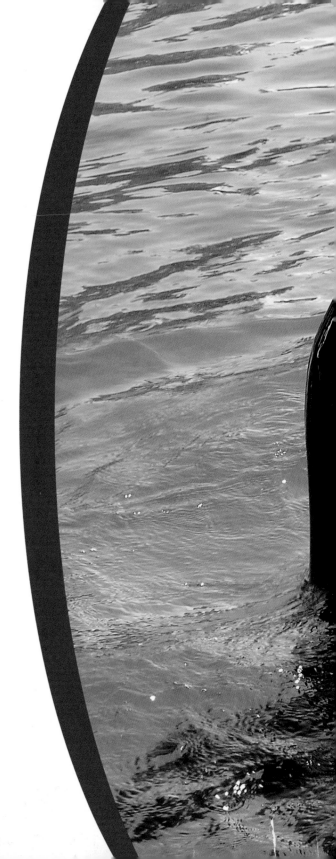

They have two fins at the ends of their tails. These fins are called flukes. They use their flukes to swim.

They have two **pectoral fins**.

They use these to steer and stop.

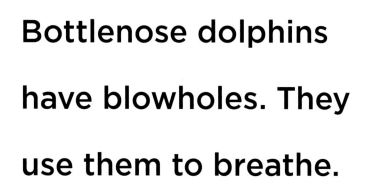

Bottlenose dolphins have blowholes. They use them to breathe.

## Helpful Friends

Bottlenose dolphins form close **bonds**. Sometimes a **pod** member can be sick or hurt. Other members help it.

18

19

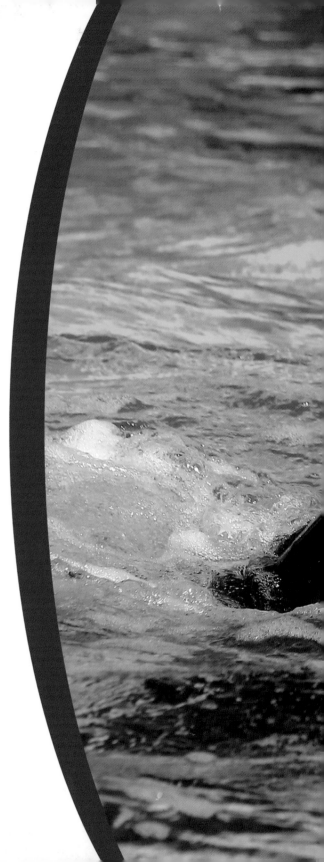

They swim beneath the sick dolphin. They push the dolphin to the surface. This is so the dolphin can breathe. They do this until the dolphin is strong again.

20

## More Facts

- Bottlenose dolphins can hold their breath for up to 7 minutes!

- Bottlenose dolphins can never fully go to sleep. They have to stay awake to breathe. They rest one side of their brains at a time.

- Bottlenose dolphins like to play. They swim in the waves. They even use their blowholes to make bubble rings.

# Glossary

**bond** – something that is shared between a group that forms a connection between them.

**pectoral fins** – a pair of fins just behind the head used for steering.

**pod** – a group of dolphins that spends most or all of its time together.

# Index

# abdokids.com

Use this code to log on to abdokids.com and access crafts, games, videos, and more!

Abdo Kids Code:
ABK8928